This Book Belongs To:

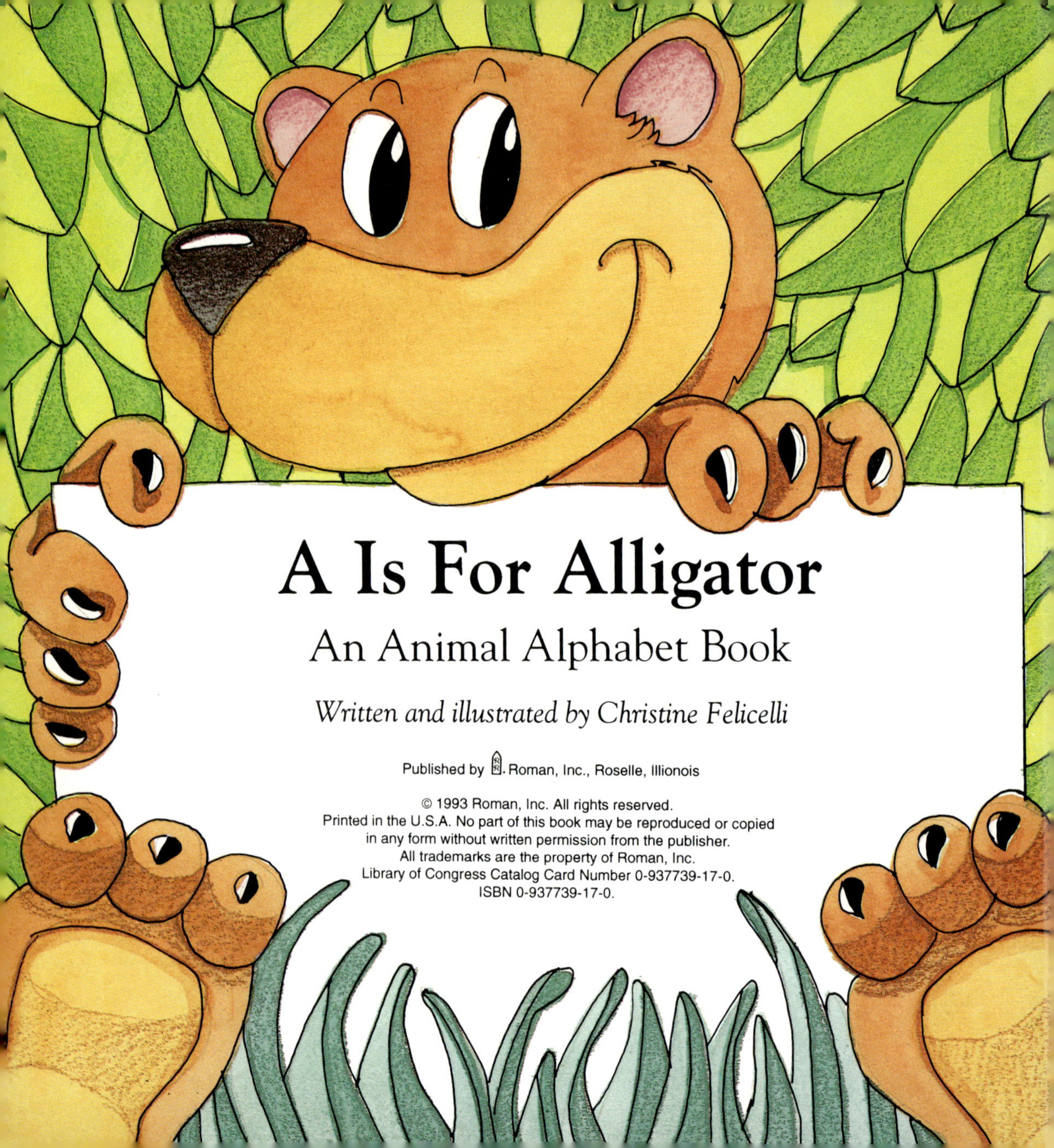

A Is For Alligator

An Animal Alphabet Book

Written and illustrated by Christine Felicelli

Published by Roman, Inc., Roselle, Illionois

Library of Congress Catalog Card Number 0-937739-17-0.
ISBN 0-937739-17-0.

Is For Alligator

An Animal Alphabet Book

Written and illustrated by Christine Felicelli

Alvin the Alligator Aches through and through.
He did Acrobatics 'til the late Afternoon.

Bernard the Bear is Behind a tree.
He eats Bright Berries, and Begs honey from Bees.

Clorindo the Cat Conspires with a mouse.
They Creep and they Crawl all through the house.

Delavan the Dog Devours his bone.
He Dives at the Door when he thinks someone's home.

Ernest the Elephant sports Enormous Ears.
He juggles Elegant Eggs, Enchanting his peers.

Ferdinand the Frog Frequently eats Flies.
He would rather Find Figs to bake in his pies.

Gustav the Goat climbs to Great heights.
Eating Green Grass is his Grandest delight.

Haversham the Horse Hops Happily on His way.
Whenever He's Hungry, He eats oats and Hay.

Ivan the Iguana lounges each day.
Drinking Ice tea and catching some rays.

Jeremy the Jaguar Jogs with ease.
He Jets and he Jumps between all the trees.

Kasey the Kangaroo bounds through the air.
She Keeps joey close, when she goes anywhere.

Leonard the Lion Likes to roar very Loud.
When he Lets Loose, he draws a Large crowd.

Mildred the Manatee Munches food from the sea.
She likes to Make Muffins with Moss and algae.

Nicholas the Newt lives Near a creek.
He dives in at Noon, at least twice a week.

Oswald the Owl Observes passersby.
On special Occasions he flies high in the sky.

Petunia the Porcupine Picks Pansies for a crown.
She dances and Prances until she falls down.

Quincy the Quail likes to waddle along.
When he's Quite happy, he sings a sweet song.

Russell the Raccoon Rests during the day.
He Runs and he Romps the whole night away.

Simon the Sea lion Seems happy and free.
He loves to eat fish that Swim in the Sea.

Toulouse the Tortoise is a very nice fellow.
He has a Tough shell with spots of bright yellow.

Ursula the Umbrella bird Uses feathers for shade
(Usually near where her eggs are laid).

Vincent the Vole is a Vivacious little mouse.
He Views the Valley below from his Very small house.

Winston the Wolf Waits under some trees.
He Winces When he feels the cold Winter breeze.

Xavier the Xiphosuran is happy as can be.
He plays the Xylophone beneath the deep blue sea.

Yolanda the Yak climbs mountains so tall.
She Yodels and listens to hear her own call.

Zachary the Zebra runs fast- Zip!
He visits the Zoo, and has fun on his trip.

THE END